When *Jesus* Speaks
to a
Grad's Heart
CLASS OF 2015

Emily Biggers

A Devotional Journal

BARBOUR BOOKS
An Imprint of Barbour Publishing, Inc.

DO NOT WORRY

Do not be anxious about anything, but in every situation,
by prayer and petition, with thanksgiving, present your requests
to God. And the peace of God, which transcends all understanding,
will guard your hearts and your minds in Christ Jesus.
PHILIPPIANS 4:6–7 NIV

When you are anxious, remember that I have not moved. Where there is confusion, I long to give you clarity. I want to replace your worries with My peace that passes all understanding, peace that cannot be found in the world but only through a relationship with Me. If you don't sense Me near, it is because you have temporarily lost your focus. I am still here. I am the same yesterday, today, and tomorrow. Look to Me. Fix your eyes upon Me. Rest awhile in My presence. Lean in a little closer. Trust Me. I've got this. I have it all under control. Do you know that I will not let you go? All the powers and forces of the world and of the spiritual realms cannot tear you away from My embrace, for I am yours and you are Mine. Leave your worries for Me to manage. Cast your cares before My throne of grace. I love you. I am here.

Jesus, I cast my cares at Your feet,
for I know You care for me. Amen.

PLANS FOR GOOD

"For I know the plans I have for you," says the LORD. "They are plans
for good and not for disaster, to give you a future and a hope."
JEREMIAH 29:11 NLT

You may not know what tomorrow holds, much less a month or a year from now. That is okay. You don't have to know. *I* know the plans I have for you. *I* see the future, and it is just right for you. I have a bright future for you. Certainly, there will be bumps along the journey. You will run into obstacles and experience setbacks. These trials will make you stronger.

Did you know that tiny turtles on the shores of a mighty ocean must struggle into the sea from the place where they are hatched? If they don't work their muscles, if someone picks them up and delivers them to the water, they will die. It is the individual journey through the sand that strengthens these creatures. Then they are ready to face the ocean's waves. You are much the same. You must face the future, all of it—glorious mountaintops but also dark valleys. You will grow stronger every day. Eventually, after you have looked up a thousand times over and found Me right there at your side. . .you will begin to trust Me more. Then you will proclaim to all who will listen that I am faithful. You will relinquish control to the One who has good plans for you.

Savior, You know the plans, and that brings
me comfort. Lead me, I pray. Amen.

BE AN EXAMPLE

Let no one look down on your youthfulness, but rather in speech, conduct, love, faith and purity, show yourself an example of those who believe.
1 TIMOTHY 4:12 NASB

I n the big scheme of things, you are still very young. Some will not take you seriously at this age. Some will laugh at your big dreams. Others may say that one day you will understand. They may believe that when you grow older, you will slow down and realize you cannot change the world. Don't waste your time arguing with them! Many have proven the scoffers wrong in My name. Young people like Timothy have become fine leaders. Focus all of your energy on standing firm in your faith. Prove to the world that you belong to Me. Be mature enough to speak with kindness, to live a life known for integrity. Love those that no one else wants to associate with, those outcast and alone, those who are hopeless. This is how I walked. This is how I lived on earth. I was your example. Now, even in your youth, be an example for others. Be found faithful when you are tempted to stray. Be found pure when your sinful nature would lead you beyond the boundaries I have established for you. Do not worry about what others think. Just live each day, each moment for Me. I believe in you.

Although I am young, Lord, I pray that You will use me in mighty ways for Your kingdom. Amen.

BE FOUND FAITHFUL

Whoever can be trusted with very little can also be trusted with much, and whoever is dishonest with very little will also be dishonest with much. So if you have not been trustworthy in handling worldly wealth, who will trust you with true riches?
LUKE 16:10–11 NIV

I want to bless you in great ways. I want you to do wonderful things for My kingdom. The world is full of distractions and false treasures. Keep your eyes fixed on Me and walk in My ways. Where you find blessing in your life, ask how you can be a blessing to others through it. If you are blessed financially, give of your money. You will find no greater joy than learning to joyfully give it away in My name. If you are blessed with talents and skills, seek opportunities to use them for Me. What I entrust to you, use wisely. I long to fill your storehouses to overflowing with every good and perfect gift. If you are faithful in the small things, I will know that you are a man or woman I can trust with much more. Hold loosely to the things I give you. They are tools, not treasures to store up on earth where rust and moth will soon destroy.

Jesus, find me faithful in the small things, that You may trust me with more each passing day. Amen.

WITHOUT LOVE. . .

*If I speak in the tongues of men or of angels, but do not have love,
I am only a resounding gong or a clanging cymbal. If I have the gift of
prophecy and can fathom all mysteries and all knowledge, and if I have
a faith that can move mountains, but do not have love, I am nothing.*
1 Corinthians 13:1–2 niv

A man who speaks in every tongue known on the earth and in heaven but has not love is worthless to Me. He is just a clanging cymbal or a resounding gong. Can you hear him? Listen. He rattles on and on. He loves to hear himself talk. He thinks highly of himself. Perhaps he speaks of Me. It is possible that he knows the scriptures backward and forward. He may sound impressive, but he does not impress Me. If he has not love, he is nothing. There are times to speak, and there are times to be quiet. It is so important to learn the difference. Pray for sensitivity to others. It has been said that everyone you meet is fighting a battle. You do not know what others are going through, so treat them all with kindness. Where you see a need, meet it. Where you can help, do so. Be known for love and for action in My name, not for grand words that sound good but bring no glory to your Lord.

*Jesus, I ask that You grant me discernment
as to when I should speak and when
I should remain quiet. Amen.*

YOUR SHEPHERD

He tends his flock like a shepherd: He gathers the
lambs in his arms and carries them close to his heart.
ISAIAH 40:11 NIV

A s you go out into this big world, there will be times when you are afraid. Something will knock you off your feet. You will realize you have strayed from Me, and you will wonder how you got into a certain situation. You will look to your left and your right and there will seem to be no escape. You will worry that you are all alone. Remember in those times that I am your good shepherd. You are My sheep. You know My voice. Listen for it. Listen for the still, small voice of your Savior. I will always beckon you home no matter how far you may wander. My voice will call to you all the days of your life. It is my desire that you walk closely at My side. My staff is near to protect you and guide you. If you walk closely, you will be able to discern My voice from the others in this world. I will gather you up close to My heart where you belong. I am yours and you are Mine.

Jesus, keep me from wandering. Draw me close to You.
I need You to be my Good Shepherd. Help me to easily discern
Your voice from the other voices in this world. Amen.

LOVE AND FAITHFULNESS

Your lovingkindness, O LORD, extends to the
heavens, Your faithfulness reaches to the skies.
PSALM 36:5 NASB

You may stay close to home after you graduate. You may travel far from the places you have known all your life to an unknown land. Wherever you go, I will be there. There is no place on earth where you can roam that I will not be faithful to you. It is My nature to be faithful. It is impossible for Me to be anything but loving and loyal to you, child. You are the object of My affection. I have redeemed you for Myself. I offer you abundant life on earth and eternal life with Me. Look into the skies. Gaze upon the mighty ocean. You cannot see an end to these. This is My faithfulness to you. This is My love. Both are without end. I am here in every season of your life, holding you close. Look to Me for guidance, for wisdom, and for comfort. I will be your Provider and your Prince of Peace always. I will bring you home to Me one day. That will be a glorious homecoming. Even in death, I am faithful, for death has lost its sting through My death and resurrection. I love you, child, with a love that goes on and on.

Jesus, Your love cannot be compared to that of
any other. Thank You for loving me. Amen.

WORK AS UNTO THE LORD

In all the work you are doing, work the best you can.
Work as if you were doing it for the Lord, not for people.
COLOSSIANS 3:23 NCV

Remember for whom you work. You will have supervisors and bosses in your work on earth. Honoring them is important. God has put them in authority over you. However, remember that first and foremost, as a Christian, you represent Me. In all things, in all situations, in all environments. . .you are Mine, and others are looking to you as an example. Work to the best of your ability. Avoid laziness. Be the employee who can be counted on, the worker who goes the extra mile. Be the one who does the job right rather than halfheartedly. When there are opportunities to be dishonest, choose honesty. Where there are ways to slip by producing less, give more. Be trustworthy. Work as unto Me and you will be blessed. Something different will be seen in you because you are a child of the living God. You will stand out. You will find favor with your employer just as Joseph did in the palace of the pharoah.

Lord, help me to work to the best of my ability.
Help me to honor You in my work. Amen.

LOOK FOR THE ESCAPE

No temptation has overtaken you but such as is common to
man; and God is faithful, who will not allow you to be tempted
beyond what you are able, but with the temptation will provide
the way of escape also, so that you will be able to endure it.
1 CORINTHIANS 10:13 NASB

A bite of fruit in the garden changed everything. Sin entered the world. Temptation is all around you. Satan lurks about like a lion, just waiting, longing to devour that which belongs to the King of kings. He has no power over you. In My name, and if you draw upon the strength that is yours through Me, you can overcome temptation. You are tempted in the same ways that other men and women before you have been tempted. The world calls out to you, but you do not have to answer its call. There is a higher call on your life, child. You answer to the Creator of the universe. You are empowered through your Savior. So, when you are tempted, look up. Look up. Look out. Look for the way of escape that I provide for you. Flee from sin. Your rewards will be great. When you are tempted, it will never be beyond what you and I can handle together if you will just look up.

Jesus, be my strength as I fight temptations in my life.
Teach me to look up and to find the way
of escape that You provide. Amen.

A GOOD WORK

For I am confident of this very thing, that He who began a good work in you will perfect it until the day of Christ Jesus.
PHILIPPIANS 1:6 NASB

You are a work in progress. You are growing every day, though. You have learned from your mistakes. You are pressing on toward the goal, the prize that is yours in salvation. I will never give up on you. I have told you that nothing is able to separate us—nothing on the earth and nothing in the heavenly realms. Satan does not have the power to snatch you from My grasp. You are Mine, and I will continue to perfect the good work I have begun in you until I come back to take you to heaven. Keep looking to Me. Fix your eyes on Mine. I will hold your gaze. I will direct your steps. I will fulfill you as nothing in the world can do. We will walk together hand-in-hand. I will use the trials and tribulations that you face to teach you valuable lessons. I will be there when you fall to pick you up and set you on stable ground again. I do not expect perfection from you, My sweet one. I only expect devotion. Look to Me. I will perfect you in due time. Your righteousness before your God is found in Me.

Jesus, help me not to beat myself up for failing. I recognize that I am not perfect. Continue working on me, Lord. I want to be more like You. Amen.

STRENGTH IN CHRIST

*"Do not fear, for I am with you; do not anxiously look about you,
for I am your God. I will strengthen you, surely I will help you,
surely I will uphold you with My righteous right hand."*
ISAIAH 41:10 NASB

D o not be afraid. Do not fret. I am with you. Not only am I with you, but I hold you up in my righteous right hand. The same hands that crafted the universe hold on to you. The power that raises the ocean's waves and thunders in the heavens has a strong grasp on your life. I am your strength. You need no other source. What problem do you wrestle with day and night? What sin binds you? What looms in the future that frightens you? Whatever it is, lay it down today. Cast your cares before My throne. Empty your hands. You hold so tightly to these worries when I desire for you to find freedom. I want you to raise your hands in worship. Let Me have hold of the concerns. I am big enough to handle it all. I am sure and steadfast. I am the Lord your God. I will never waver in My love for you.

*Jesus, I feel like I am slipping. I do not feel steady. Please hold on
to me. Hold me up with Your righteous right hand today. Amen.*

CHRIST'S RIGHTEOUSNESS

He made Him who knew no sin to be sin on our behalf,
so that we might become the righteousness of God in Him.
2 Corinthians 5:21 nasb

———————————

You are enough just as you are. I have covered your sin with My righteousness. I could not value you more than the day I saved you. You are imperfect, but you are perfectly Mine. God does not see the filthy rags that are your sin when He gazes upon you. He sees you through the lens that is His Son. He sees you through Me, and He sees you as righteous. In My righteousness, you are fully accepted, fully saved, fully loved. Rest in Me, and know that your good works, while pleasing to Me, are not what saves you. You are saved by grace through faith. You are made white and spotless through the Lamb. God made a way for you, and you have chosen it. You have chosen well. You have surrendered. Now each day of your life, go out into the world and shine your light before men. There are so many working, working, working. . . They scramble and toil in order to win the favor of others. . .the favor of God. Show them the way, for you have learned the truth and the truth has set you free.

———————————

Savior, thank You for being my righteousness before God. Amen.

SELF- VERSUS OTHERS-CENTERED

*Do nothing from selfishness or empty conceit, but with humility of mind
regard one another as more important than yourselves; do not merely look
out for your own personal interests, but also for the interests of others.
Have this attitude in yourselves which was also in Christ Jesus.*
PHILIPPIANS 2:3–5 NASB

It is natural to look out for yourself. However, you are not natural. You traded natural for supernatural when you asked Me to take up residence in your heart! You invited the Savior of the world to come in and clean house! I have found smudges here and there that appear to be self-centeredness. I see cobwebs of covetousness that need to be cleared. Let's clear them away, you and I. I will help you to see others the way I see them. Instead of looking to your own interests, think of those around you. What are their needs? What causes that sharpness in her tone of voice? What makes him react defensively? Where can you sow seeds of peace? Where can you touch with the tenderness that I have shown you, even in your sin, even in your imperfection? Love as I have loved you. Forgive as I have forgiven you. Replace looking out for self with looking out for others. You will be amazed at the joy this brings.

*Lord, give me what it takes to get my focus off of self
and onto others. I want to love as You love. Amen.*

YES IN CHRIST

For no matter how many promises God has made,
they are "Yes" in Christ. And so through him the
"Amen" is spoken by us to the glory of God.
2 CORINTHIANS 1:20 NIV

The promises of God are too vast and too deep for your human mind to conceive. They are promises made with you in mind. They are for your good and never to harm you. They are promises from a holy, sovereign heart of love. There will be times when your prayers seem unanswered. There will be times when the answer is no. In those times, though you are tempted to give up on God, hold fast. I am the fulfillment of the promises of God. All of His promises find their "yes" in Me. Every "no" that God speaks leads to a time when your Abba Father is pleased to say yes. Yes, My child. Yes, here is a good gift. . .worth the wait, worth some struggle and pain. It is a magnificent word: *Yes.* Walk in His ways. No turning back. Find every promise of God kept completely at the foot of the cross. The Cross of Calvary where I laid down My life for you. God loves to bless His children. Trust Him.

Jesus, You are all I need. When the answer is no, give me the endurance
I need to press on toward the prize, which is my Savior. You are the
ultimate fulfillment of every beautiful promise of God. Amen.

SECURE IN CHRIST

No, in all these things we are more than conquerors through him who loved us. For I am convinced that neither death nor life, neither angels nor demons, neither the present nor the future, nor any powers, neither height nor depth, nor anything else in all creation, will be able to separate us from the love of God that is in Christ Jesus our Lord.
ROMANS 8:37–39 NIV

Insecurity raises its head again and again in your life. You feel it, don't you? It may look a little different, but it is the same each time, a reminder of your humanity. You walk in fear instead of peace. You look to your left and your right when your eyes need to remain fixed on Me. Bring it to Me. Toss your insecurity at the foot of My throne. Like a child at play who deposits a jacket on her mother's lap and skips away unencumbered, bring it to Me. Look into My loving eyes. Find Me faithful. I've got your back. Find security in your relationship with Me. You have a new name. You are more than a conqueror through Me! Even on days when you have to drag it—a heavy trunk filled with weight too great to lift—bring it to Me. This is a task you must be committed to, child, for all of your life you will be tempted to believe that you are not good enough, that you don't have what it takes. I stand strong and ready to help you. You must choose to lay down your insecurity. We can do this, you and I.

Thank You, Lord, that in You I am eternally secure. Amen.

STRENGTH SOURCE

But he said to me, "My grace is sufficient for you, for my power is made perfect in weakness." Therefore I will boast all the more gladly about my weaknesses, so that Christ's power may rest on me. That is why, for Christ's sake, I delight in weaknesses, in insults, in hardships, in persecutions, in difficulties. For when I am weak, then I am strong.
2 CORINTHIANS 12:9–10 NIV

Remember that power outage? You were surrounded by darkness. You stumbled over furniture. Then a generator did its job. Another source gave you light. The churning of its workings was loud and powerful. It kicked in when you were helpless. It provided light, and once again you walked steadily.

I am your source. My grace is enough. You are weak, but I am strong. See weakness as a blessing, My child. Look it in the face. Fear it not. Like the apostle Paul, delight in weakness. Call it what it is, and seek your Strength Source. I stand ready to help you. In your hardships, I carry you. When others insult you, I remind you of your great worth. When you are persecuted for your faith, look up. The Object of your faith supports you. I am your Anchor, your Guide. I will lead you in paths of righteousness beside still waters. My rod and my staff will protect you and steer you clear of danger. I am sufficient for every need.

Jesus, in my greatest weakness, I find Your greatest strength. Amen.

RESCUE

Answer me, LORD, out of the goodness of your love;
in your great mercy turn to me. Do not hide your face
from your servant; answer me quickly, for I am in trouble.
PSALM 69:16–17 NIV

I am your rescue. When sin overwhelms, cry out to Me. When others misunderstand or hurt you, call on Me. In weakness, find strength. In insecurity, find stability to anchor you again in your faith. I do not answer you because of your ability or your perfection. I answer you because I am yours and you are Mine. When I hear that you are in trouble, I rush to rescue you. I promise to provide a way out when you are tempted. I delight in comforting you when your heart is sad. It is My deep desire that you should look to Me in times of struggle. I will pull you through not once or twice, but every time. There is no limit to My love for you. There is no place you can go that is too far. There is no sin too awful for Me to forgive. There is no depth of depression where My mercies cannot reach you. My mercies are new every morning. My heart is for you, never against. Call on Me. I am here for you always. I am your Good Shepherd. You are My beloved little lamb.

Thank You, Lord, for rushing to my
rescue when I need help. Amen.

PRAISE HIM

*Why, my soul, are you downcast? Why so disturbed
within me? Put your hope in God, for I will yet
praise him, my Savior and my God.*
PSALM 42:5 NIV

It is easy for you to praise Me on the mountaintop. The skies are blue there. The sun shines. And all is well. What about when you find yourself in a valley? A dark one. One that is empty, where you feel all alone. Do you praise Me there? Will you? When depression has a grip on you and sorrow fills your days. . .will you put your hope in Me? Will you praise Me still? David was pursued by his enemies. He knew how it felt to try to hide horrendous sin. He was betrayed by his own flesh and blood. David was not on the mountaintop when he penned this psalm. He was in a dark, dark place. His spirit was downcast. His mind was disturbed. Yet he knew Me. He knew that his God was a big, big God. He made a conscious decision back there somewhere on a mountaintop that he would praise Me in the valleys. Then, when he was in one, he remembered the commitment.

Make that choice today. Be ready. There will be days that you will need to have a plan for praise in your back pocket. Praise Me still. I am worthy of worship every single day of your life.

Savior, I will praise You. Amen.

DESTRUCTION VERSUS LIFE

The thief comes only to steal and kill and destroy;
I have come that they may have life, and have it to the full.
JOHN 10:10 NIV

As you step into this new chapter of your life, remember that I desire an abundant life for you. Eternal life does not begin when you enter heaven. It began the moment you accepted Me as your Savior. I have great plans for you, a bright future, blessings that you cannot even imagine. Tap in to the source of joy and contentment that is available to you through My Word. Come to Me in prayer. Walk with Me. I will never lead you astray. Satan is a deceptive thief, and because I love you, I will not sugarcoat this truth—he wants to devour you. He will tempt you in subtle ways, and if you are not walking closely with Me, you may give in to his lies. The thief will take from you, but I will only give. No good and perfect gift will I withhold from My own. When I say no or when I discipline you, it is for your good and never to harm you. I love you with an everlasting love. I want you to live life and live it to the full. Live your life in such a way that it brings glory to God.

Lord, protect me from the lies of the devil.
Draw me close. I want to walk with You. Amen.

CALL UPON JESUS WHEN IN TROUBLE

"Call upon Me in the day of trouble; I shall
rescue you, and you will honor Me."
PSALM 50:15 NASB

When you were an infant and you cried out in the night, a parent or guardian came to you. He or she lifted you from your crib and held you. You were comforted. Your needs were met. If you were hungry, you were fed. If you were wet, a clean diaper solved the problem. As a child, when you had a bad dream, you called out in the night. A cool drink of water and a hug made it all better. You are older now. You are stepping out into unknown territory. There will be trouble there; there is trouble in this world. Yet you know how to call out. Apply that in your prayer life. When you are in trouble, call on Me. When you are afraid, I will be your Prince of Peace. When you find yourself in turmoil, call upon Me. I am a first responder. I am the only response you need. I will drop everything and come to your aid. Call upon the name of your Savior. You are never too far from My reach. You are never too deep in trouble for Me to scoop you up and bandage up your wounds. That is My job. I love you.

Thank You for being there for me on good
days and bad days alike, Jesus. Amen.

EVERY DAY

Praise the Lord; praise God our savior!
For each day he carries us in his arms.
PSALM 68:19 NLT

There are many things that come around once a year or so. Vacations. Holidays. Birthday parties. Yet I am with you every day. When you are victorious, I cheer on the sidelines. When you stumble, I rush to your side. On good days, find Me in the sunshine. On bad days, look for a rainbow among the clouds. I am there. I am always, always there. You will find Me at the party. I am celebrating with you but also reminding you of whose you are and how you should conduct yourself as a believer. You will find Me in the exam room as the doctor delivers news that shakes you—a diagnosis you never expected. You will find Me as you ponder big decisions that loom before you. Where will you live? What job will you accept? Do you say yes or no to a certain relationship? You will find Me there because I am an everyday Savior. I don't just show up every other weekend like a dad with partial custody. I am in love with you, and I can't stay away. You are My heartbeat. Nothing brings Me greater joy than to walk with you and guide you through this life until you are with Me in paradise.

Jesus, thank You for being an everyday Savior. Amen.

WHAT A SPIRIT!

For God has not given us a spirit of fear and timidity,
but of power, love, and self-discipline.
2 TIMOTHY 1:7 NLT

D id you hide behind your mother's legs as a child? You were too shy to speak to the adults to whom she was attempting to introduce you. You hid from them, or at least tried to hide from them. Then your mother said, "Come out, child. Look them in the eye. Say hello." She took your hand. She assured you that it was okay. In her strength, you spoke. You found the ability to do so as she encouraged you and stood with you. She was familiar, a protector. She was yours. The same is true of your Holy God. Through My death on the cross, you have access to Him. He fills you with strength. He is the source of all love, and it flows freely through you. You are not like those of this world who do whatever feels good. You are a strong horse, but with a bridle. I have drawn sweet boundaries for you. Be disciplined in your reading of My Word. Be controlled in your passions and desires. In this you will find freedom and joy. Remember today to whom you belong and the spirit of power He has placed in you.

Lord, I am strong in You. I love because You first loved me.
I will seek to be self-disciplined. Help me, I pray. Amen.

A VOICE BEHIND YOU

Whether you turn to the right or to the left, your ears will hear
a voice behind you, saying, "This is the way; walk in it."
ISAIAH 30:21 NIV

The coach is on the sidelines. He shouts out directions. He calls the plays. He reacts with elation or anger, depending on how things go. I am right behind you. I don't call to the team. I speak to you individually. I am not a reactor but your greatest fan, regardless of how the score looks. When I see you making a decision that will lead you astray, I beckon you back to the path of righteousness. Are you listening? Don't tune Me out, child. Your focus must not be on an electronic device or an earthly relationship. Your eyes must be fixed upon Me. I will hold your gaze. I will not look away. Your ears must not be so attuned to the music blasting through your headphones that you miss Me. I am your Good Shepherd, and you are My lamb. My sheep know the voice of their very own Shepherd. They hurry to follow My commands. They heed the touch of My staff as I guide them in the way they should walk. They have learned to trust the Shepherd. Do as these little lambs. Trust in Me. I will provide a way out, a route to peace, a road that leads you to pleasant pastures.

Thank You, Jesus, that I hear Your voice. You are my Good Shepherd. Amen.

FACING TEMPTATION

Because he himself suffered when he was tempted,
he is able to help those who are being tempted.
HEBREWS 2:18 NIV

Y ou will face new temptations as you step into this chapter of your
life. As an adult, you will have more freedom, but with that comes
danger. What choices will you make? You will be tempted in your work—
to be lazy, to do as little as possible. It is an option but not the best one,
not the godly one. Choose to work as unto the Lord and not as unto mere
men. You will be tempted to compromise in relationships with the opposite
sex. Going too far physically will always lead you down a path of emotional
turmoil with which you are not meant to deal. Follow My ways. Save sex
for marriage. You will find blessings beyond measure when you do it My
way. The world's way is counterfeit and empty. I want the fullness of the
real deal for you, child. Trust Me in this. You will be tempted to stretch the
truth. There is no peace in lies. You will be drawn to worldly pleasures that
promise it all but deliver destruction. I was tempted, too. Satan mocked
Me. Look Satan in the eye, dear one. Tell him you belong to the Messiah.
Tell him no. He will shrink back when he hears My name. There is power in
the name of your Savior.

Lord, help me to resist temptations and the tempter himself. Amen.

DO NOT SIN IN ANGER

*"In your anger do not sin": Do not let the sun go down while
you are still angry, and do not give the devil a foothold.*
EPHESIANS 4:26–27 NIV

Anger is a part of life. Even I was angry when I walked on earth, but I was without sin. In My power, you can do likewise. I will give you the strength to resist sin. Take a deep breath. Count to ten. Whisper a prayer. Step away. Surrender. Have you found that things look better in the morning? Don't say in the nighttime what you will regret when the sun comes up in the morning. Remember that the tongue is a double-edged sword. It can speak Life, but it can also wound another's heart deeper than any man-made weapon. The tongue can cause great destruction that is hard to undo. Watch your words. Control your reactions. When you do have disagreements, find a way to settle them before the sun goes down for the day. Going to bed angry never benefitted a marriage or a friendship. Bitterness grows quickly. It provides a foothold for Satan. It gives him something to cling to as he attempts to scale the walls that keep him from your heart. Your heart belongs to Me. Don't give the devil a route into what I have claimed for God's glory! Resist the devil. In your anger, do not sin.

*Jesus, be my strength. I do get angry. Keep me from
sinning against You in such moments. Amen.*

FORGIVEN

"I, I am the One who forgives all your sins, for my
sake; I will not remember your sins."
ISAIAH 43:25 NCV

D o you take back gifts you have given to others? When you give a Christmas or birthday gift, do you then try to pry it out of the recipient's hands only to have it for yourself again? Of course not! Nor do I. I give forgiveness as a free gift. Through your faith in Me, by grace, you are saved. Your sins are forgiven. That includes your past sins, those you will commit today, and the sins in your future. You are washed clean by the blood of the Lamb. I made a way for you to come before a Holy God. So when you have asked Me to forgive you, accept My answer. Yes, child, I forgive you. Don't try to bear the burden of guilt any longer. That is My burden now. I gladly bear it for you. Don't treat Me as one who would snatch back My gift once you have opened it and begun to enjoy its benefits. I forgive you. I have forgotten your sins. I tell you in My Word that I have cast them as far as the east is from the west. That is not an empty promise; it is one you can take to the bank.

Thank You, Lord, for forgiveness of sins. Help me to accept forgiveness
from You, and give me what it takes to truly forgive others. Amen.

A HEART OF FORGIVENESS

*So, as those who have been chosen of God, holy and beloved,
put on a heart of compassion, kindness, humility, gentleness
and patience; bearing with one another, and forgiving each
other, whoever has a complaint against anyone; just as
the Lord forgave you, so also should you.*
COLOSSIANS 3:12–13 NASB

The fruits of the Spirit are yours because you belong to Me. The Holy Spirit empowers you to be kind, humble, gentle, and patient. The Spirit guides you and gives you strength to be self-controlled. Certainly the sin nature is still at work, but through your relationship with Me, you can choose to put on a heart that clearly loves others. As you spend time in My Word and in prayer, your heart softens. As you experience My grace, you will want to show grace to others. When you recognize how patient I am with you, you will be patient with those around you. As a recipient of kindness and blessings, you will begin to show kindness to your neighbors. You are chosen by God. You are His precious child. He could not love you any more than He already does. They will know you are a Christian by your love. Love others well. In doing so, you reflect the love of My Father.

*Lord, soften my heart. Show me how to forgive
the way You have forgiven me. Amen.*

CHOOSING FRIENDS

One who has unreliable friends soon comes to ruin,
but there is a friend who sticks closer than a brother.
PROVERBS 18:24 NIV

C hoosing friends is tricky business. You are in the world, but you are
not of it. As you graduate and move into the next phase of life, you will
make new friends. These may be people you work with, go to graduate
school with, or meet in your community. One great place to meet friends
is at church. Other people who are seeking to know Me better make good
friends. I don't call you to surround yourself only with other believers.
I was a friend to Zacchaeus and to Levi. I befriended a woman who had
had five husbands and who was living in sin. Yet I do want your close
confidants to be Christians. Fellow believers share your worldview. They
see life through the same lens that you have been given. They will give wise
counsel when needed and stand by you through thick and thin. The goal is
not to be popular and to have many friends. The goal is to carefully select
a few in whom you will invest and in whom you can trust. I chose twelve
for My inner circle, and then I served and loved the masses. Follow My
example. Choose your friends wisely.

Help me, Jesus, to be discerning as I choose close
friends to do life with day by day. Amen.

PROTECTION FROM THE EVIL ONE

*But the Lord is faithful, and he will strengthen
you and protect you from the evil one.*
2 Thessalonians 3:3 niv

You are a child of the God of angel armies. When you call out to Him, He will put a hedge of protection around you. He will send His angels to guard you. In your weakness, through your faith in Me, you can find great strength. When you come to the end of yourself, you have come to a wonderful place. It is there that you will look up and realize the amazing power of your God. Satan may tempt you, but ultimately he has no power over you. He would love to lead you astray, but you are held in God's hand.

Nothing is able to snatch you away from your Father. *Nothing.* When you are afraid, lean in to God. When you are weak and you feel yourself swaying to the devil's schemes, speak My name. There is power in My name, and it will cause Satan to shrink back like a wounded puppy. He has no choice but to flee when a believer tells him to in the name of Jesus. You will not be harmed. You will stand strong in the face of temptation. The God of angel armies will see to that.

Protect and strengthen me, I pray. Amen.

JESUS IS WITH YOU

Lift up your eyes and look to the heavens: Who created all these? He who brings out the starry host one by one and calls forth each of them by name. Because of his great power and mighty strength, not one of them is missing.
ISAIAH 40:26 NIV

The world is a big place. It seems so inviting until you cross that stage, receive the diploma, and head out into it. This can be an overwhelming step! You may feel alone. . .and very small. You are making decisions that will impact your future—where to live, a career path to follow, and if you will marry. You are forging new roads, leaving behind norms established while in school. There was safety in those old routines.

Now change is unsettling. Take heart in the knowledge that I am with you. Just as I placed the stars in the sky and know them by name, I know you. Not in part, but fully. You are known through and through by your Creator. I have not forgotten nor will I ever leave you. You are always within My line of vision. I love you beyond measure. Look into the night sky. Gaze upon the vastness of space and the bright twinkling stars, each one in its place. With the same strength that holds the universe together, I hold on to you. Together we will face your future. You are never alone.

It comforts me to be known by my Savior. Go with me, Jesus, as I step into an uncertain future. Amen.

ENCOURAGE ONE ANOTHER

Therefore encourage one another and build
each other up, just as in fact you are doing.
1 Thessalonians 5:11 niv

Are you an encourager? Everyone needs encouragement. Throughout the ages, I have set My people in place to build one another up. Barnabas encouraged Paul; and Paul, in turn, encouraged Timothy. Exhortation is not the spiritual gift of all believers, but all can participate in it.

You can grow as an encourager. Start simple. Speak an uplifting word to another Christian today. Think about that individual. What can you say that will spur him on toward good works for the kingdom? What do you see in her life that inspires or makes an impression on you? Point it out. Speak Life into the darkness of this world. When you do so, you diminish the enemy's discouragement in that life. Encouragement is not flattery. It is genuine and heartfelt. You may never know the impact of your simple word of encouragement. It is like a cup of cold water to a parched traveler.

Encourage your pastor and church staff. They are under attack every day. Urge younger or less mature Christ-followers to continue reading the Word and spending time in prayer. Be known as a helper and a supporter because encouraging others is part of My purpose for you.

Jesus, help me to be an encourager today. Show me someone
who needs to be built up in the Lord. Amen.

GOD MEETS YOUR NEEDS

And my God will meet all your needs according
to the riches of his glory in Christ Jesus.
Philippians 4:19 niv

G od is bigger than you can imagine. He created the world and put the stars in the sky. Every animal, every flower, every tree. . .was by His ingenious design. And He made you. He knit you together in your mother's womb, in the secret place. Through My sacrifice upon the cross, God is able to meet all of your needs. The bridge between sinners and a Holy God was formed by the cross. God is able to meet not just some, but all of your needs. When you are lonely, He is there. He will provide for your physical needs, and He will protect your mind and heart. You have to ask. He stands ready to help you. He longs for that opportunity. As you grow in your walk with Him, your desires will change. Once you may have asked God for material things, but you will find yourself crying out to Him for the salvation of lost souls. Once you asked Him for a relationship, but you will begin to thrive in your relationship with Me as Savior and Friend. An earthly relationship is just an extra blessing. It is not something you need or must have in order to navigate this life. God is nonnegotiable. He is to be your all in all. Let Him meet your needs.

Lord, meet my needs, even needs I don't
know I have. I love You. Amen.

PEACE

God is not a God of confusion but a God of peace.
1 CORINTHIANS 14:33 NCV

———————————

Just as I am your King of glory, I am also your Prince of peace. There is no price tag that you can put on peace. It is invaluable, priceless. Peace cannot be bought by the wealthiest men in the land. There is no counterfeit for it. It is either present or absent, filling you up or unable to be found. When you lay your head on your pillow at night, you should rest in complete peace. Ask Me for this. I want nothing more than to grant it. I will not lead you in a way of confusion or distress. My paths are clear, and while not always easy, they are always peace-filled. When you are walking in My ways and about My purposes, you will know it. Your heart will be at rest. Your mind will not be troubled. I offer you peace that the world cannot give, peace that comes only through Me. If something you are doing does not line up with the Word of God. . .you will not experience peace. As a believer, you have the Holy Spirit as your Counselor. He will never lead you away from God, but always toward Him. Be sensitive to the Spirit. Seek peace with your whole heart. It will be well worth your quest.

———————————

Grant me peace in these moments, Jesus.
Fill me to overflowing with peace. Amen.

TRUST IN THE LORD

Trust the LORD with all your heart, and don't
depend on your own understanding. Remember the
LORD in all you do, and he will give you success.
PROVERBS 3:5–6 NCV

Sometimes you will not understand My ways. In such times, you must trust Me. Don't depend on what you can see before your face. Sometimes you must simply walk in faith. Faith is trusting in what is not seen. Faith is grasping that you don't have to know everything because you are held in the hand of One who does. You know that I love you and that I always have your best interest at heart. As you walk through life, especially now that you are out of school, you will not be able to rely on knowledge or routines. You must rely on Me. When you start that new job, remember Me in your work. Acknowledge that every good and perfect gift comes to you from My hand. The job itself was not earned or attained, but given to you as a blessing, as a means of earning a living, and as a mission field. As you climb the ladder, take Me with you. Never go ahead of Me. Never forget who got you there. I will give you success. Give Me the glory.

Jesus, keep my eyes always fixed on You. You are my
life. Help me to trust in You and to acknowledge that
there is no success aside from what You give. Amen.

PERSECUTION

But if you suffer because you are a Christian, do not be ashamed. Praise God because you wear that name.
1 PETER 4:16 NCV

S tephen was the first martyr for the Christian faith, and I stood from My throne at the right hand of the Father to welcome him into heaven. Stephen was not ashamed of the Gospel. He spoke the truth in love, but he was hated for his words. He was stoned to death, and yet, as his spirit entered paradise, he asked God not to hold his murderers' sin against them. I spoke those same words about those who crucified Me.

You will suffer for My name. If you are never persecuted or scorned for your beliefs, perhaps you need to be bolder for Me! When you are laughed at for the things you will not do, remember Daniel, who would not deny his God. When you are scoffed at for following God's call on your life, remember Noah, who constructed an ark on sunny days. Do not be ashamed of suffering in My name. Wear the name "Christian" with thankfulness, for you have been saved from eternal damnation by that name. God has given you a new name. You are more than a conqueror.

Jesus, forgive me for sometimes wanting to blend in with the crowd. Help me to be bold for You in this world, and if I meet with opposition, help me to stand up for what I believe in. Amen.

GOD-CENTEREDNESS

For where jealousy and selfish ambition exist, there is disorder and every evil thing. But the wisdom from above is first pure, then peaceable, gentle, reasonable, full of mercy and good fruits, unwavering, without hypocrisy.

JAMES 3:16–17 NASB

There will always be someone who seems to have what you want, someone who has a better job or relationship, someone who appears to have it all together. Learn to be happy for others, but not to covet what they have. Be interested only in My will for your own life. When you are looking out for number one, you miss out on My blessings. When you focus on Me, you will rest in contentment with what I have given you. When you love and serve others, you will be so blessed. Seek wisdom in all things, the wisdom that comes only from Me. It cannot be found in this world. When you seek wisdom, I will give it to you. Then you will find peace. You will demonstrate gentleness and mercy to those around you. You will be levelheaded in your thinking, and your feet will not falter. You will walk a straight path. You will not waver in your faith. Lay down jealousy, and trade self-centeredness for God-centeredness. This is My desire for you.

Turn my focus from self to others.
Change my jealousy into joy, I ask. Amen.

TREAT OTHERS AS YOU WISH TO BE TREATED

*Treat others the same way you
want them to treat you.*
LUKE 6:31 NASB

I t is called the Golden Rule. You learned it as a child on the playground or in school. Your parents may have emphasized it during periods of sibling rivalry in your home. You are older now, out on your own, living your own life. Are you applying the Golden Rule, or have you forgotten it lately, passed it off as "kid stuff"? Are you generous with grace? Do you stand in judgment of others, or do you see them through a lens of mercy, the way I gaze upon you? Are you known for encouragement and service, or are you known for a critical spirit? It is good to examine your heart from time to time. Are you truly treating others as you want to be treated?

Be extravagant with forgiveness and with grace. This will bless those around you who will never measure up. They are sinners, as are you. They are imperfect, but they have great value in God's economy. They are His greatest creation, His masterpiece—humans. Treat them kindly. Look for the good in them, not the bad. Build them up rather than tearing them down. Follow the Golden Rule. It is God's will for your life.

*Jesus, help me to see and treat others as I should.
Give me an extra measure of Your grace and mercy
that I might live out the Golden Rule. Amen.*

A NEW THING

"Forget the former things; do not dwell on the past.
See, I am doing a new thing! Now it springs up;
do you not perceive it? I am making a way in the
wilderness and streams in the wasteland."
ISAIAH 43:18–19 NIV

Where there seems to be no way, I will make a way. Don't look back. Look forward. If you have repented, that which you regret is gone—I have cast it as far as east is from west. You are not forgiven partially, but completely. Let it go. Do not dwell on the person you once were. Rearview mirrors are handy for driving, but not for life. Look forward. Don't you see it? I am at work in your life. You are a new creation.

I am making a way for you. If what you need from Me seems impossible, remember that I am a God who regularly does the miraculous in the lives of His children. I am not limited by human boundaries, and I love to bless you. If you cling to the past, you will miss the present, and therefore, you will forfeit your future. I have so much more for you than that!

Take My hand. Let's move forward. Let's walk through the wilderness on a clear path. Let's drink deep from a cool stream in a land that was once only desert. I have a bright, beautiful future for you. It begins today.

Jesus, thank You that You do not dwell on
my past. I am a new creation in You. Amen.

PHYSICAL HEALTH

Dear friend, I pray that you may enjoy good health and that all may go well with you, even as your soul is getting along well.
3 John 1:2 niv

I care about your physical health. I want you to feel well and enjoy abundant life. I have put twenty-four hours into each day, and you need to rest at least eight of those. Sleep is so important to your well-being. You were not made to work around the clock. When the earth was created by God in the beginning, it was filled with vegetation of all types. There are so many healthy fruits and vegetables that are delicious and also good for you. As a Christian, there is no food that is unclean for you to consume. If you choose, eat meats that will provide your body with protein and energy. There will be times when your body is not well. You will be sick. This is because you live in a fallen world. One day there will be no more sickness, no more death. One day you will be with Me in paradise. For now, your body must face attacks of disease. When you are ill, take care of yourself. See a doctor. Rest. Do the things that are necessary to become healthy again so that you may be about your heavenly Father's business in the world.

Lord, bless me with good health. When I am sick, help me to slow down and take care of myself. Amen.

CONTENTMENT IN CHRIST

The Lord is my shepherd, I lack nothing. He makes
me lie down in green pastures, he leads me beside
quiet waters, he refreshes my soul. He guides me
along the right paths for his name's sake.
PSALM 23:1–3 NIV

Contentment is learned. It is not your human nature to be satisfied. You have been saved, but still there is a sinful nature at work within you. It battles with your new nature as a believer. It tells you that you need this or that in order to be happy. Satan lurks about and wants to deceive you into believing that I am withholding good gifts from you. He did this in the Garden of Eden with your ancestors. He told Adam and Eve that they were missing out. He clouded their contentment with doubt. He seduced them away from satisfaction and offered them an opportunity. They believed him. They sold out.

Tell the devil to flee from you. When he whispers that there is more, that you can have it, that he has something you want, something you need. . .remember that snake in the garden. He is still alive and well, and he is a cunning one. Find your contentment in Me. I am all you will ever need. On your best day and your worst, your soul can find rest and delight in your salvation. I am your Shepherd, and you lack no good thing.

Thank You, Lord, for contentment and peace. Amen.

GIVING

"Give, and you will receive. You will be given much. Pressed down,
shaken together, and running over, it will spill into your lap.
The way you give to others is the way God will give to you."
LUKE 6:38 NCV

B e a cheerful, generous giver. Give until it hurts. Give beyond what you think you can or should. You can never out-give Me. Test Me in this. Bring to Me your tithe, give even beyond it. I will prove to you again and again that I am Jehovah-Jireh. I am your Provider. Give of your money, but give also of your time and talents. I gifted you at the time of your salvation with spiritual gifts. You may have one gift or many. Determine what these are. Study your temperament, your abilities, and your leanings. If you are merciful, be extravagant with mercy. If you are a teacher, teach the Good News with passion. If your gifts are those of helps or administration, put them to use for My kingdom. Your spiritual gifts are for the building up of My Church, not for your own use, not to be tucked away for another less busy day. They are to be poured out as a fragrant offering to your King. Give of your gifts. You will never be disappointed in giving. Try Me. And when you find Me faithful, tell others. You simply cannot out-give Me.

Jesus, make me a cheerful giver and one
who gives naturally and freely. Amen.

GOD'S WORD IS LIGHT

*Your word is like a lamp for my
feet and a light for my path.*
PSALM 119:105 NCV

Have you ever walked through a dark field? You needed that flashlight to guide your steps, didn't you? Without it, you would have been lost and in the darkness, you would have been fearful. It is the same in life. You need a guide. You need light in the darkness. This world has many options for paths you can take. It will offer you any number of routes that will bring nothing but disappointment and destruction. Walk in the light you have been given as a believer in Me. You have been given the Holy Scriptures. They are alive and sharper than a two-edged sword. The commands within the pages of the Bible are for your good. The guidelines are to ensure peace and joy in your life. If you have not opened your Bible in a while and dust is forming on it, open it today. Spend some time in prayer and in meditation on the scriptures. They are like food for your body, living water for your weary soul.

*Thank You, Lord, for the Bible. It is light in the darkness.
It guides me in truth. I desire to walk in the path
of Your commands for my life. Amen.*

SALVATION

But God shows his great love for us in this way:
Christ died for us while we were still sinners.
ROMANS 5:8 NCV

I didn't wait. I didn't ask you to clean up your life to be worthy of My sacrifice. I walked the road to Calvary beneath the weight of an old rugged cross. It was not pretty. It was heavy and splintered. It was all I could do to drag it up the hill. That cross had your name upon it, and it was not the nails but your sin that held Me there as they crucified Me. I didn't wait until you were clean. No, I became your purity, allowing you access to the Father. I didn't ask you to make yourself a little better. I died for you while you were still a sinner. Your good works were as filthy rags. They did nothing for you. Your righteousness comes only as a result of faith placed in Me as Savior. God sent Me into the world to save sinners. I am the bridge between His holiness and man. I did it. I saw that it was the only way. The cup did not pass from Me. I drank deeply of it. My blood poured out as atonement for your wrongdoing. In that moment, once for all, grace won. Unmerited favor. Undeserved compassion. Unimaginable substitute. I died for you. Live for Me.

Jesus, thank You for providing life for me
through Your death upon the cross. Amen.

APPROACH THE THRONE WITH CONFIDENCE

Let us then approach God's throne of grace with confidence,
so that we may receive mercy and find grace
to help us in our time of need.
HEBREWS 4:16 NIV

When you come before Me, you may do so with confidence. I will always be ready to show you mercy and grace. You can't earn it or pay for it. You can't do enough good works to receive it. My grace is a gift. My mercy is a natural overflow of My deep love for you. You have received Me into your heart and made Me your Savior. You are daily learning more about making Me Lord of every area of your life. You are sealed with the Holy Spirit, a child of the Living God, saved by grace. Come to Me. Ask for what you need. Pour out your heart. Cast all your concerns at the foot of My throne. I care for you, and I always will. There is no sin too great to change how I feel about you. There is no road you can go down where I will not be ready to welcome you back home. Don't come to Me as a stranger. Come as a child to a parent. Come as one dear friend to another. Come to Me. I long to cover you with grace and mercy.

Jesus, thank You that I find my confidence in You.
You are my Savior and my Lord. Amen.

HONOR THE LORD WITH YOUR BODY

Do you not know that your bodies are temples of the Holy Spirit, who is in you, whom you have received from God? You are not your own; you were bought at a price. Therefore honor God with your bodies.
1 CORINTHIANS 6:19–20 NIV

Your body is not your own. Such a concept sounds utterly crazy to a nonbeliever. As a Christian, your body is the temple of the Holy Spirit. You are a living, breathing witness to the grace of your Savior. You have been made different. You are set apart. You were bought with My blood poured out on the cross, and you belong to a sovereign God. I bore your sin—all of it—past, present, and future. I died that you might have life. Because of grace, do you just sin all the more, knowing you will be forgiven? No! To experience an abundant life on earth, you must surrender your fleshly desires to Me. You must day by day, sometimes hour by hour, come before Me and ask Me to give you strength to resist temptations of the body. Sexual temptation is extremely strong. If you have not already faced this, you will. It may seem overpowering at times. Yet I always provide a way out, an escape. Flee the sins of the body, for your body belongs to the One who saved you.

Lord, help me to maintain purity, and help me not to sin against You or others with my body. Amen.

THE LORD NEVER SLUMBERS

He will not let you be defeated. He who guards you never sleeps.
He who guards Israel never rests or sleeps. The LORD guards you.
The LORD is the shade that protects you from the sun.
PSALM 121:3–5 NCV

I am a strong tower, your refuge, and I never change. I am not like the shifting sands. I never slumber. I am always watching over you, protecting you. I have set My angels around you many times that you do not even know about. I have held back that which would have destroyed you. Each breath you take is known by Me. Each step you take is directed by Me. I never, for one moment, look away. If you wonder why bad things have happened to good people, listen. . . It is a fallen world where you make your temporal home. Life on earth is but the blink of an eye. It is just a warm-up, a dress rehearsal for heaven. Satan is alive and well in your world. Sin results in death.

Death will come to every human. It may have seemed to come too soon to some that you knew and loved. Death for the believer is but a transfer from abundant to eternal, from earth to glory. I do not take My eyes off My children. I love you with a constant love. Nothing touches you that does not first pass through the filter of your Savior.

Jesus, I can rest easy knowing that You never sleep.
You are always watching over me. Amen.

LIVE IN PEACE

*It is good and pleasant when God's
people live together in peace!*
PSALM 133:1 NCV

Y ou are called to live at peace. This is a high calling, but it is the one
you must live out as a believer. When the world looks at the Church,
it will never find perfection. Since the fall in the garden, sin has existed.
No man, not even a wonderful anointed pastor called to share the Good
News, is perfect. Yet when the world looks at the people of God, it should
see a reflection of the heavenly Father's love. It should find joy within
the walls of the Church. It should sense that there is a peace about these
people. If there is turmoil within the Body of Christ, how is this different
from the world? The earth is filled with chaos. Christians are to be set
apart. A different worldview causes Christ-followers to approach personal
relationships differently. You must be humble in order to live at peace with
others. You must surrender your will to that of the Father. You must turn
from self-centeredness. Even when you want to fight for your cause, even
when you just know you are right and the other party is wrong. . .you must
surrender. Peace must rule in your mind and heart. You must daily seek
strength from Me in order to live at peace with others.

*Jesus, let me be known as a peaceful person.
Help me live at peace with other believers. Amen.*

WHEREVER YOU GO

*If I rise with the sun in the east and settle in the
west beyond the sea, even there you would guide
me. With your right hand you would hold me.*
PSALM 139:9–10 NCV

No matter where you go, I am there. As you graduate and make
changes, you may find yourself in a new location. I am already there.
I have gone ahead of you. I have prepared friends for you. I have a Church,
a body of believers for you to fellowship with. There are blessings awaiting
you in this new place. You must seek Me, and I will be found. Throughout
your life, I will guide you. I will hold on to you as a parent holds the hand of
a child. I will keep you close because you are Mine.

If you stay close to home or if you are led to a distant land makes
no difference. I am in the sunrise in every nation. You will find Me in
the crashing waves of the Pacific and the Atlantic. I will pursue you in
faithfulness. You need only to allow Me to be your guide. You need only to
seek Me, and I will be found.

*Lord, go with me all of my days. It is a great comfort to know
that You are with me wherever I may live and work. Amen.*

SLEEP IN PEACE

I go to bed and sleep in peace, because,
L<small>ORD</small>, only you keep me safe.
P<small>SALM</small> 4:8 <small>NCV</small>

I don't like to see you tossing and turning in your bed at night. I want you to rest easy. You are in My care. I never sleep or slumber. When you abide in Me, you can rest assured that I will watch over you.

Cast your cares on Me, and let Me do the work. You are not meant to bear such a stressful load. If you are worried about the future, remember that I am your Provider. I am in your job, schooling, and relationships. I am aware of all of your needs. There is no human that can take on your burdens the way in which I am able. I alone can keep you safe. I alone can handle all of your worries with great ease. There is nothing too big for Me.

Nothing, absolutely *nothing*, is able to keep Me from you. You are saved from sin and from the world. You are not aimlessly wandering through a dry desert land. You have the chance to live life to the full. An abundant life and peaceful rest in the goodness of your Savior are blessings I offer. Receive them, child.

Jesus, as I lay my head down to rest, remind me that
You are sovereign. You watch over me and guide me. Amen.

ASK GOD FOR WISDOM

*But if any of you lacks wisdom, let him ask of God, who gives to all
generously and without reproach, and it will be given to him.*
JAMES 1:5 NASB

What troubles you today? What decision are you desperately trying to make? Where is there confusion or turmoil in your life? If you need wisdom, you need only to ask. True wisdom cannot be found in the world. It must come from above. The sooner you learn this in life, the better off you will be. Don't run from friend to friend bending their ears and asking them for their opinions. Resist the urge to analyze day and night until you find the answers. They will not come by this method. You have tried this before, remember?

Learn to turn quickly to your heavenly Father when you need understanding, when you must make a choice, when you need wisdom. Just as earthly parents give generously to their children, I long to pour out wisdom upon you. Just as I did not force My way into your heart, I will never push My ways on you. I am patient, longing for you to come before Me and ask for My thoughts to become your thoughts, My will to become your will. You must be transformed through the renewing of your mind. When you seek wisdom, it will be found.

*Jesus, I need wisdom for the decisions I must
make today. Guide me in Your ways. Amen.*

STRAIGHT PATHS

*Listen, my son, accept what I say, and the years of your life
will be many. I instruct you in the way of wisdom and lead
you along straight paths. When you walk, your steps will
not be hampered; when you run, you will not stumble.*
PROVERBS 4:10–12 NIV

T he world is full of crooked paths. When you take these roads, you will stumble and fall. Certainly, I will be there to pick you up again and set you straight. Yet why continue to make the same mistakes again and again? Why would you choose to wander on paths that lead to nowhere, routes where the final destination is destruction? If you walk in My ways, I will make your paths straight. There will not be roots that grow up and cause you to trip. There will be only smooth, clean roadways. This doesn't mean that trials will not come to you, but you will continue to walk in My ways with the prize set before you. I am the prize. I am the object of your heart's desire. Don't confuse that desire with the empty promises the world makes. I am the Way, the Truth, and the Life. I offer you a road that leads to Life. Take My hand, and I will lead you on the way that leads to glory.

*Lord, set me straight on the path that leads to Life.
When I wander, call out to me. Don't let me stray too far. Amen.*

LEARNING TO WAIT

Wait for the LORD; be strong and take
heart and wait for the LORD.
PSALM 27:14 NIV

Y ou wait in lines every day. You have done it all your life. As a child, you waited your turn to go down the slide on the playground. As an adult, you wait to order food at the drive-through, to purchase groceries, and to see the doctor. You have become accustomed to waiting.

Yet, you find it hard to wait for Me. You want what you want, and you want it now. Sometimes My answer to your prayer is yes, child. Sometimes it is no. Still other times, My answer is wait. That is perhaps the most challenging of the responses. Waiting requires trust and patience. It requires you to have faith that I am working behind the scenes.

When life seems boring and uneventful, rest in the knowledge that I have not ignored or forgotten what you have asked Me for. I love you. I want the very best for you in every area of your life. I am deeply interested in your career, your friendships, your mate, your dreams. But sometimes I will ask you to wait. There is always a reason. There is a purpose in the plan. Good comes from learning to wait. Wait for Me. I am never early or late. I am always right on time in your life.

I trust You, Lord. Help me to wait upon
Your plans and Your answers. Amen.

DEALING WITH ANXIETY

Cast all your anxiety on him
because he cares for you.
1 PETER 5:7 NIV

Anxiety is not from Me. Come to Me in prayer, and present to Me your requests. Be thankful in all circumstances, but don't be afraid to come to Me and pour out your heart. Wringing your hands will never solve anything. I have a vast supply of wisdom. I am interested in every detail of your life. I want to guide you in the ways that are the very best for you. Not just good, but the best. When I knit you together in your mother's womb, I ordained every day that you will live on earth. I already had plans for you. I have great purposes for you, purposes that will bring Me glory, plans that will impact My kingdom. I do not see you as small. You have great value, grand significance to Me. You are more than a conqueror through Me. You have power and ability when you call upon My name. There is no problem too perplexing, no struggle too strong, and no issue too complicated for Me to tackle for you. Seek Me. Pray earnestly. I want you to lay down those anxious thoughts. I want to take them from you, but you must hand them over to Me, child.

Lord, sometimes I cling to my problems. I find it
hard to lay them down. Help me to
trust You more. Amen.

BE HONEST ALWAYS

Yes, always use honest weights and measures, so that you may enjoy a long life in the land the LORD your God is giving you.
DEUTERONOMY 25:15 NLT

Honesty is important. When you lie, it becomes a habit. Small lies turn into larger ones. Soon you feel you must lie to cover up another lie. Your life becomes a tangled web of deceit. That doesn't sound appealing, does it? That is no way for a child of God to live.

As you leave the safety net of school and find yourself with more responsibilities in your work and in life, choose honesty. It is always the best policy. It will help you to find favor with your employer. One day you may be the employer. Being honest in all your dealings with them will cause your workers to trust you and to be faithful to you.

Being honest is something that cannot just start when you are put into a position where a white lie could get you out of trouble temporarily or benefit you in some way. Determining to be honest is a commitment you must make before you are in that situation. It is something you must resolve within yourself as My disciple. Represent Me well in the world through your character. Be honest.

Jesus, give me an honest heart. I want to honor You in this way. Amen.

WORK IS GOD'S DESIGN FOR YOU

*The LORD God took the man and put him in the
Garden of Eden to work it and take care of it.*
GENESIS 2:15 NIV

W*ork* is not a bad word. It is My desire that you should work. From
the beginning, work was a good thing. Adam and Eve were to
work in the Garden of Eden. Their work was pleasant. After the Fall, work
became more difficult. Because you live in a world where sin resides,
you will experience toil and the stress of work overload. However, work is
not a bad thing. You were created to work.

Six days the Father worked at creating the world, but on the seventh
He rested. You were designed for work but also for rest. When you find
yourself leaning to one extreme or the other—there is danger. Look out.
Laziness and idleness will lead you to destruction very quickly. On the
other hand, if you work yourself to death, you will ruin your relationships,
and your life will count for nothing but constant labor. Find the balance.
Seek wisdom from Me. I want to show you how you can be blessed through
your work.

*Lord, help me to find the balance between work and rest.
I want to be pleasing to You in my work. Amen.*

THE BIG PICTURE

Yet God has made everything beautiful for its own time. He has planted eternity in the human heart, but even so, people cannot see the whole scope of God's work from beginning to end.
ECCLESIASTES 3:11 NLT

Y ou have worked a puzzle. Remember how it feels to look at the pieces scattered across the table? It is overwhelming to put the puzzle together if you can't see what it should look like in the end. I have the final picture in mind. I see all the pieces of your life, and I see the outcome. I see the beautiful image of your perfected faith. I see the souls that will be saved because you answered My call to share your faith. I see the tasks that you will accomplish, tasks ordained for only you to accomplish. There is a time for everything.

Don't be anxious when things do not happen in your time. My timing is perfect. I reveal to you what you need to know for each day. If a door closes in the job world or a relationship comes to a screeching halt, do not look to your left or your right. Look to Me. It simply was not time. That does not mean a promotion won't ever come. That does not mean you will not be given a faithful spouse. It means that you must submit your will to Me. You must accept with grace that I have the timing under control.

Lord, I so long to see the big picture! Help me to trust in Your perfect timing. Amen.

CHILD OF THE LIGHT

For you are all children of the light and of the day;
we don't belong to darkness and night. So be on your guard,
not asleep like the others. Stay alert and be clearheaded.
1 Thessalonians 5:5–6 nlt

———

Y ou are in the world but not of it. Heaven is your home. You are but an alien on the earth. Because you belong to Me, you must be on guard. Satan is alive and well in the world. He seeks to devour and destroy that which is of the Light. You must resist temptations to become drunk on alcohol or put substances in your body that alter your thinking. Drugs and alcohol will cause you to do things you would not otherwise do. You must be alert and clearheaded in order to resist the temptations of the devil. You are of the day, not the night. You are a child of the Light, not the darkness. The Light has overcome the darkness, but you must choose daily to tap in to the power source that is yours in your walk with Me as your Savior. A child of the Light will never be satisfied walking in darkness again. You have experienced walking in the Light. Submit to Me daily, and find Life in the Light.

———

Jesus, remind me to whom I belong. I want to represent
You well in the world. I want to be salt and light
to everyone I encounter. Amen.

FRUIT OF THE SPIRIT

*For this very reason, make every effort to add to your faith goodness;
and to goodness, knowledge; and to knowledge, self-control; and to
self-control, perseverance; and to perseverance, godliness; and to
godliness, mutual affection; and to mutual affection, love.*
2 PETER 1:5–7 NIV

———

The fruits of the Spirit are yours through your salvation. The Holy Spirit wants to add these traits to your life. Faith requires action. To be known as a child of the King, you must put on the full armor of God every day. You must be prepared to give an answer for your joy. You must be ready to share the Gospel. You must be a reflection of the Father to the world.

The fruits of the Spirit will set you apart. When you are self-controlled, others will wonder the source of your strength. Godliness is not always attractive to the world. You may be persecuted or scoffed at, but you will be respected. In the end, you will be the one that others come to for advice. They will run to you for counsel. The world will know that you are a Christian by your love. Show brotherly love to all believers. Agree to disagree. Live at peace with them. This is your offering to the heavenly Father. This is His calling on your life.

———

*Lord, may the fruits of the Spirit be evident in my life. May I be known
for these things—goodness, knowledge, self-control, perseverance,
godliness, mutual affection, and above all. . .love. Amen.*

REJOICE IN SUFFERING

...through whom we have gained access by faith into this grace in which we now stand. And we boast in the hope of the glory of God. Not only so, but we also glory in our sufferings, because we know that suffering produces perseverance; perseverance, character; and character, hope.
ROMANS 5:2–4 NIV

I love to see you rejoice. When you smile, I smile down upon you from heaven. I delight in blessing you with good gifts. Every good and perfect gift in your life has come from My hand—every relationship, every position, every material possession. It is all from Me.

There are times, though, when you must suffer. The world is not a perfect place. There will be hardships. I know firsthand. I experienced them when I walked on earth. I was fully God, but I was also fully man. I understand every temptation, heartache, and disappointment.

When you face suffering, you must count it as joy. This is a calling on your life as a Christian. You must not wallow in self-pity when you are disappointed. When you experience loss and defeat, look to Me. Remember My promise that I work all things together for good for those who love the Lord. Suffering produces perseverance in you. Perseverance develops your character. Then character produces hope.

Lord, it is easy to rejoice in victories. Help me to rejoice even in my sufferings, for I know they draw me closer to You. Amen.

HAVE FAITH

*He regarded disgrace for the sake of Christ as of greater value
than the treasures of Egypt, because he was looking ahead to
his reward. By faith he left Egypt, not fearing the king's anger;
he persevered because he saw him who is invisible.*
HEBREWS 11:26–27 NIV

C hristian, you are called to walk by faith. Faith is trusting in what is
not seen, what is invisible to the human eye. You know that I am
here. You must trust Me. I am always at work for your good. When you
begin to doubt that you will get a job, have faith in Me. When you feel that
you cannot handle yet another breakup, look to Me. When you have no
place to live, remember that I did not have a home when I walked on earth.
Trust Me as your Provider. I will not lead you astray.

When you are in a new place and feel alone, trust Me. Find your hope
in Me. Seek My face. I want to encourage you to simply speak My name in
the face of uncertainty. There is power in My name. When you feel afraid
or unsettled, cling to your faith. It will become easier the more that you
practice this. I can see that which you cannot. Walking in faith is a daily
decision. Each day remember that I am in control. Take My hand and walk
in faith with your Savior.

*I have faith, Lord. Make it stronger.
Increase my trust in You, I pray. Amen.*

OTHERS' INTERESTS

Don't look out only for your own interests,
but take an interest in others, too.
PHILIPPIANS 2:4 NLT

It is easy to get caught up in looking out for number one. Do you find yourself chasing your own dreams at the expense of others? Do you make conversation, or do you ramble on and on about your own desires or problems? Remember to look to the interests of others as well. In My ministry on earth, I modeled this for you. I healed the sick and preached to the crowds. I noticed the woman at the well and met her deep need for Living Water. I walked with the Twelve and taught the masses. I touched the leper. I called forth Lazarus from the grave and turned his sisters' grief to joy. People are My heartbeat.

You will find great freedom when you let go of self-absorption and focus on those around you. I put people on your path every single day with whom you can interact and love. Even a smile, a kind word, or a simple act of kindness can make all the difference in another's life. Don't look only to your own interests. Look to the interests of others. This is My command.

Jesus, I want to be more like You each day.
Help me to take my eyes off my own needs and worries.
Help me to put others above myself today. Amen.

THE HOLY SPIRIT

*"You fathers—if your children ask for a fish, do you give them
a snake instead? Or if they ask for an egg, do you give them
a scorpion? Of course not! So if you sinful people know how to
give good gifts to your children, how much more will your
heavenly Father give the Holy Spirit to those who ask him."*
LUKE 11:11–13 NLT

Regardless of your relationship with your earthly father, know that your heavenly Father's heart is always for you. It is never against you. He loves to give you good gifts and bless your life and see you smile.

Even human fathers know how to love their children. They provide for their children. The Father has given you the Holy Spirit. We are three in one, the Trinity. It is hard for you to comprehend, but we are singular and unique, yet one in the same.

The Spirit is your Comforter, your Counselor. You do not have to beg the Father for the Spirit. You are sealed with the Holy Spirit at conversion. You have access to the Spirit's peace, and you have been given discernment through the Holy Spirit's indwelling of your heart. Draw upon this power. You need the power of the Holy Spirit. More important than food and water to sustain your body is the Spirit's strength to sustain your soul.

*Lord, I pray that I will be sensitive to the
work of the Holy Spirit in my life. Amen.*

EQUALLY YOKED

*Do not be yoked together with unbelievers. For what
do righteousness and wickedness have in common?
Or what fellowship can light have with darkness?*
2 CORINTHIANS 6:14 NIV

Your closest relationships are to be with other Christians. There is no other way around it. You are asking for trouble if you choose otherwise. I chose twelve men as My inner circle. They are known to you as the twelve disciples. Even within this group, there was one disciple whom the Bible says was the one I loved. Certainly I loved them all. I love all people and wish that none should perish. This one was a special friend to Me. There was a special place in My heart for John. Have you found that friend who is closer than a brother? Do you date nonbelievers, or are you convinced that My Word is true? I tell you that you should not be yoked together with someone who does not share your worldview. As a Christian, you are set apart. The way you walk and talk and make decisions is different from the way an unbeliever does these things. You have nothing in common with someone who does not cherish Me as Savior. Certainly you are to be in the world. I am not calling you to isolate yourself. Be among non-Christians. Fellowship with them. Lead them to Me. But your closest relationships should be with Christ-followers.

*Lord, help me to make sure that my closest relationships
are with people who share my love for You. Amen.*

THE IMPORTANCE OF CHURCH

You should not stay away from the church meetings, as
some are doing, but you should meet together and encourage
each other. Do this even more as you see the day coming.
HEBREWS 10:25 NCV

S ome will say that they meet with Me on the fishing boat or in their living room. They say they do not need church. They may find fault with the church, calling its people hypocritical or judgmental. I tell you to find, meet with, and build community with your local church. The Church was My idea, not man's. I have established it, and it is for your good. Worshipping and serving with other Christians is an irreplaceable blessing in your life. Do not neglect it. Online sermons are a wonderful tool for those who are truly unable to get to church. They do not replace what I want you to have in your church home. I want you to have a family there. The Church is made up of all different kinds of people, but they have one very important thing in common: they know Me as Savior and seek to know Me better. Find a church. Get plugged in. Stay plugged in. You will be blessed in this.

Lord, lead me to the church You have for me.
I want to meet with Your people and be a part
of something bigger than myself. Amen.

SPEAK THE TRUTH IN LOVE

Faithful are the wounds of a friend,
but deceitful are the kisses of an enemy.
PROVERBS 27:6 NASB

Speak the truth in love, and be ready to hear correction from a trusted friend. If you cannot be open and real with Christian friends, with whom can you do this? You need accountability. You were not created to be alone. You were designed for fellowship with Me and with one another. When you see a Christian friend going astray, speak Life over him or her. Speak the truth, but do it with kindness, not for your own gain or out of pride. It may not be exactly what your friend wants to hear, but to stand by and watch this person walk down a road that leads to destruction is not kind or loving. Likewise, be open to constructive criticism. Ask a godly friend or two to be ready to speak into your life as they see a need. You have been blessed with friends. Do not neglect this important aspect of Christian companionship. Speak the truth. . .always in love. Always be ready to receive it.

Jesus, show me a friend to whom I can be
accountable, one who can be accountable to me
as well. I need this type of openness in my life. Amen.

OWE ONLY LOVE

Owe nothing to anyone except to love one another;
for he who loves his neighbor has fulfilled the law.
ROMANS 13:8 NASB

L ove is the greatest of the three—faith, hope, and *love*. Love never fails. It keeps no record of wrongs. It endures. It stands the test of time and perseveres under hardship. It is not self-centered, but looks to the interests of others. Love is patient, gentle, and kind. Love held Me on the cross as I bled and died and emptied Myself that you might be filled to overflowing. . . Love is a hug, a kiss, a kind act. It is a feeling—but so much more. It goes far beyond emotion. Love is not about what you can get, but rather how much you can possibly give—a little more each day. You fulfill everything the Father calls you to if you learn this one thing. Love with extravagance. There was a woman who could not help herself but to pour expensive perfume upon My feet. She humbled herself to use her hair to wipe My feet. She was scorned for wasting something that could have been sold in order to meet the needs of the poor. Yet I blessed her name! This one knew the meaning of being spilled out for another. Go and do likewise. Love with your whole heart. You may have other regrets at the end of your life, but you will never regret having loved another well.

Help me to love beyond the limits I have had in the past, Father. Amen.

MEET WITH JESUS IN THE MORNING

*In the morning, O Lord, You will hear my voice; in the
morning I will order my prayer to You and eagerly watch.*
Psalm 5:3 nasb

There is something special about meeting with Me first thing in the morning. No matter how rough things are at night, the next morning you have a clean slate, a new beginning. When the sun rises, draw near and meet with Me. Pray to Me. Acknowledge My holiness. Tell Me who I am to you. Confess your sin. Lay it before Me, and give Me the great privilege of forgiving you. Again and again I will forgive you. I know that you are weak, but as you walk with Me, you will be given strength, and I will always provide you a way out of temptation. Seek Me in the morning. Thank Me for the blessings in your life. Even if you feel disappointed, thank Me for the things that are good in your life. As you do so, you will begin to notice more of My blessings throughout each day. Finally, child, pray to Me about your needs and the needs of others so that I might help you with them. I stand ready to meet you in the morning. Let's start each day together. Let's begin with this one. I love it when you come to Me before you start your day.

*Jesus, thank You for meeting with me in the
morning. I want to begin all my days with You. Amen.*

HOW TO PRAY

And when you are praying, do not use meaningless repetition
as the Gentiles do, for they suppose that they will be heard
for their many words. So do not be like them; for your
Father knows what you need before you ask Him.
MATTHEW 6:7–8 NASB

I am not looking for fancy words when you pray to Me. What impresses Me is not your language but your heart. My eyes move to and fro across the land. My ears are attuned to My people's prayers. I love to hear you praise Me, to know that I am at the center of your life. I love to hear you call Me by name—Savior, Lord, Jesus. I don't need your words, but I delight in them. When you lift your concerns to Me and surrender them at the foot of My throne, I gather them up and handle them with care. I release you from the burden you were not meant to bear.

When you pray, don't look for a formula. Don't try to imitate someone else's method. I am simply interested in walking and talking with you. Remember not to do all the talking. Take time to be still and listen for My voice. I know your needs before you bring them to Me, but I love it when you are faithful in prayer. Prayer changes things. There is great power in prayer. Always remember that.

Thank You, Savior, for the privilege of prayer.
I am amazed that I can just sit in my living room and
converse with the God of the universe. Amen.

OVERLOOK WRONGS

Sensible people control their temper;
they earn respect by overlooking wrongs.
PROVERBS 19:11 NLT

A re you quick to forgive, or do you hold grudges? In life, people are not going to do everything according to your wishes. They are only human, just as you are. They have faults and deficiencies. It is a fallen, sinful world in which you all are making your temporary home. In heaven, there will be no offenses. There is no sin in paradise—only joy, worship, and Light.

For now, earn respect by being quick to overlook offenses. When someone wrongs you, give him or her the benefit of the doubt. Try to put yourself in the other person's shoes. Did he realize that this act would hurt you? Was that her intention? Certainly there are times to express your hurt feelings. What I am saying is that it should not be every day, every time. That is not reasonable. A sensible woman realizes when to hold her tongue. A wise man knows when to simply let it go. Overlooking wrongs should be at the top of your list in any relationship, whether it is a marriage or a friendship.

Love covers a multitude of sins. Love keeps no record of wrongs. Show grace. Emulate My great grace outpouring upon you, child. There is blessing in heaping grace upon grace on those you love.

Lord, I am quick to look out for number one. Help me to
overlook wrongs and not be so quick to get defensive. Amen.

PRAISE THE LORD

Let everything that has breath praise
the LORD. Praise the LORD.
PSALM 150:6 NIV

I f you do not praise Me, the rocks will cry out. The Lord must be praised. I long to hear the praises of My people! I am Creator, Savior, Lord. I am Redeemer of the years the locusts have eaten, your Prince of peace, your King of kings. I am the Great I Am. I am all that you need. My grace is enough. My heart beats for you. I am the Messiah, the Resurrected Jesus. Up from the grave I arose, and I now sit at the right hand of God. I reside in your heart because you invited Me in. Now what will you do with Me?

Don't put Me on a shelf in your back room. Put Me at the center of your existence. Lift up your songs to Me. I am both before and after all things. I am in all things, and through Me all of creation is held together. I am the Alpha and the Omega. I am the Trinity, three in one, Father, Son, and Holy Spirit.

Who do you say that I am? If I am all that your T-shirts and your bumper stickers claim, worship Me. Humble yourself. Escape your busyness. Find time for Me. Sing Hosanna. Welcome Me. Shout hallelujah to your King. I delight in the praises of My people. Let everything that has breath praise the Lord!

Jesus, I praise You. You are so worthy of my praise. Amen.

ONLY ONE GOD

Do not worship any other god, for the LORD,
whose name is Jealous, is a jealous God.
EXODUS 34:14 NIV

Y ou may think this does not apply to you. You don't serve other gods. Or do you? There are gods all around you. They may not look like deities, but they have become so. They may look like cell phones, computers, televisions, and even relationships. They are gods—little "g" gods. Often, they come between you and the one true God.

I am jealous for you. I love you with an everlasting love. I want nothing less than all of you. You may not be bowing down to graven images, but where are you investing most of your time? On what are you spending most of your money? Where is your mind? Your heart?

I long for your undivided devotion. I want to walk and talk with you. I want you to depend on Me, not on anything or anyone in the world but Me. I am your Creator. I designed you right down to the details of your eye color and the shape of your nose. You are precious to Me, and I will pursue you. Worship Me as the one true God. Lay aside anything that distracts you from Me.

I will worship only the one true God.
Strip away from my life, Lord, that
which competes with You. Amen.

TRANSFORMING YOUR MIND

Do not conform to the pattern of this world,
but be transformed by the renewing of your mind.
Then you will be able to test and approve what
God's will is—his good, pleasing and perfect will.
ROMANS 12:2 NIV

T he world opposes Me. You cannot expect to listen to the voices calling out to you from the world and find Me at the end of the path. You must daily draw away from earthly things and meet with Me. I did this during My years of ministry on earth. I left the crowds. I met with God. I prayed.

Renew your mind by spending time in My Word and meditating upon its powerful words. Call out to Me in prayer. Give Me your struggles. Tell Me your weaknesses. Confess sin, then turn around. The word *repent* means to turn away from your sin. Make a decision to be different in My strength. Take every thought captive to Me. When your mind is transformed and when you are thinking and acting according to My patterns, then and only then will you be able to know My will for your life. I want this for you. I want to transform you from empty to abundant, from unstable to completely secure. It takes denying the world's tug on your heart. Are you ready for the high calling of walking with Me?

Jesus, I lay aside the world. I want to be like You. Amen.

TAKE UP YOUR CROSS

Then he called the crowd to him along with his disciples and said:
"Whoever wants to be my disciple must deny themselves and take up
their cross and follow me. For whoever wants to save their life will lose it,
but whoever loses their life for me and for the gospel will save it."
MARK 8:34–35 NIV

If you are a Christian, people will know it. They will see it in the things you do and say. They will also see it in the things you don't do or say. You cannot serve two masters. Self is a strong force. It is only natural to your sinful nature for you to focus on number one. Babies come into the world crying to have their needs met, and they really never stop. Unless a life is transformed by My grace, unless a person is saved, self will reign. Yet you have given your life to Me. You have surrendered your ways and asked Me to reveal to you My will. What holds you back? What occasionally beckons you back to your old life? Whatever it is, lay it down. You must follow Me unencumbered by the weights of this world. Take up your cross, and follow Me—wholeheartedly. The cross represents death. Are you ready to crucify your old life? Put it to death, and come find life in Me.

I want to walk with You, Jesus. Help me
to take up my cross and follow You. Amen.

AN HEIR OF THE KING

*He saved us, not because of righteous things we had done,
but because of his mercy. He saved us through the washing of rebirth
and renewal by the Holy Spirit, whom he poured out on us generously
through Jesus Christ our Savior, so that, having been justified by his
grace, we might become heirs having the hope of eternal life.*
TITUS 3:5–7 NIV

Y ou are an heir, a child of the King! You were bought with a price,
purchased with My blood. I died in your place. You are a new
creation, justified by My grace, able to stand before a holy God. You are
seen through a Jesus lens. When God looks upon you, He doesn't see the
old you. Your very best attempts at righteous deeds were but filthy rags
to Almighty God. When He looks at you, He sees you through the cross.
You are made righteous through your faith. It is a simple act of trust, a
surrender, a turning from your old life to embrace all that is yours in Me.
I delight in My coheirs. I love that you have chosen to walk with Me in this
life and to abide with Me forever in eternity. I am preparing a place for you
to spend forever with Me in paradise. You are an heir who has hope. Hope
in eternal life.

*Help me to face all that lies before me as a child of the King,
eternally saved and treasured by God. Amen.*

LOVE MUCH

*"Therefore, I tell you, her many sins have
been forgiven—as her great love has shown.
But whoever has been forgiven little loves little."*
<small>LUKE 7:47 NIV</small>

There was a woman who wept at My feet. She humbly cleaned My feet with her hair and anointed them with fine perfume. People said to send her away. They said if I knew the depth of her sin, I would be appalled and wouldn't let her touch Me. How wrong they were! Those whom I have forgiven much understand grace. They are overtaken with gratitude. Those who grow up in churches with white steeples may hum hymns and quote scripture. . . They may be found inside the church's walls instead of outside of them—but I rescued them from darkness just the same. They often have a harder time grasping what forgiveness really means.

Fall before Me today. Let your sin bring you here in humility. Don't be in a hurry. Linger here at My feet, in awe, remembering from where you have come. Realize that from your birth you were sinful. Take in the fact that not one selfish attitude or impure thought can come before a holy God. You have been forgiven more than you can comprehend. You are washed as white as snow. Breathe in the goodness of the Lord! Take it in, and then go forth and love the world around you—extravagantly.

*Thank You, Lord, for saving me. Help me to love You
with my whole heart, and help me to love others
with wild abandon. Amen.*

KINDNESS IN JESUS' NAME

*"And whoever in the name of a disciple gives to one
of these little ones even a cup of cold water to drink,
truly I say to you, he shall not lose his reward."*
MATTHEW 10:42 NASB

When you serve the world in My name, you are serving Me. Simple kindnesses do not go unnoticed. As you are graduating and laying your plans for the future, do not forget about love. Remember that even a cup of cold water offered in My name is a blessing. I am pleased when you love others and show kindness. Look out for the needs of others. Where you see a need, if you are able, meet it. Don't focus on what it will do for you or what you will get out of the act. Just do it. Buy a meal for someone who is hungry. Don't contemplate his motives or his weaknesses. Dwell on the knowledge that he is a child of God, created in God's image, just as you are. Reach out to a dying world. Share the love that you have found in Me. You will never regret showing kindness. It takes just a few minutes of your day to show random acts of kindness. Do them in My name.

*Lord, sometimes I get so caught up in my own plans
for the future that I miss opportunities right under my nose
in the present. Help me to see needs and meet them. Amen.*

A SERVANT'S HEART

But Jesus called them to Himself and said, "You know that the rulers of the Gentiles lord it over them, and their great men exercise authority over them. It is not this way among you, but whoever wishes to become great among you shall be your servant, and whoever wishes to be first among you shall be your slave; just as the Son of Man did not come to be served, but to serve, and to give His life a ransom for many."
MATTHEW 20:25–28 NASB

It is natural that you want to climb the ladder of success. You may have dreams of becoming a leader in a company. You may want to become the principal of a school after teaching for a few years. It is good to have goals.

My message here in scripture is not to remain in a low position in your career. I am not telling you it is wrong to work hard to land a position of authority. My message is about your heart. When you lead, do so with a servant's heart, modeling humility and grace. Think of others first. Build them up even if you have the power to tear them down. I was sent by the Father into the world to serve, not to be served. I am your example. I have shown you love, grace, and many, many chances. Go and do likewise.

Lord, may I always remember that there is great reward in putting others first. Amen.

OBEY GOD'S COMMANDS

Loving God means obeying his commands. And God's commands are not too
hard for us, because everyone who is a child of God conquers the world.
And this is the victory that conquers the world—our faith.
1 JOHN 5:3–4 NCV

I have called you to love your neighbor. I have commanded that you serve rather than look to be served. I have taught you through My Word to be kind and generous. I call you to forgive those who have hurt you—whether they apologize or not. My commands probably sound like tall orders. Not just everyone has the strength to carry them out, but you do. You do because you do not operate in your own strength. You are Mine, and I am yours.

Through the indwelling of the Holy Spirit in your life, you have the power to love and to give. You are able to let go of deep hurts. It may take time, but you will get there. I have equipped you with a power source that is far greater than any you can find in the world. To truly love Me is to follow My commands. As you live and work and make decisions, abide in Me. Your faith in a very competent Savior conquers the world. I will reveal Myself in and through you.

Lord, I want to love You with my whole heart.
I am more than a conqueror in Christ Jesus. Amen.

PRAISE THE LORD

"Bring to me all the people who are mine,
whom I made for my glory, whom I formed and made.
The people I made will sing songs to praise me."
ISAIAH 43:7, 21 NCV

W hen was the last time you truly worshipped? I don't mean merely singing words of praise from choruses or hymns. I don't even mean raising your hands or closing your eyes. I call you to sing unto Me, to truly worship Me—with all that is within you. I see your heart. You are Mine, fashioned in My image. From the dust you were created, and My breath was breathed into you. You stand out among all of My creation. You are higher than the animals, even than the angels. You are mankind, My pride and joy, My delight. You were made for My glory. You are destined to an awesome eternity of praise.

Let it begin now. Bask in the goodness of being known, fully known, and loved still. I love you with all of My heart. I laid down My very life for you. Sing praises to Me. You will, in doing so, find sweet release. It is when you worship Me that I can apply balm to your wounded spirit. When you recklessly praise Me, I can draw close enough to ease your weary soul.

Lord, You say that if we do not worship You, the rocks
will cry out. You must be praised! Let me begin today
to worship You in a deeper way. Amen.

REMEMBER CHRIST'S WORDS

Don't ever forget my words; keep them always in mind.
They are the key to life for those who find them; they bring
health to the whole body. Be careful what you think, because your
thoughts run your life. Don't use your mouth to tell lies; don't ever
say things that are not true. Keep your eyes focused on what
is right, and look straight ahead to what is good.
PROVERBS 4:21–25 NCV

My words are the key to life. Once you hear them, don't forget them. If you give Me control over your thoughts, your words, and your eyes, I will keep you on track. You must submit to Me every day, sometimes multiple times per day. Take every thought captive to your Savior. There are many paths you could choose, but if you choose the path of Life, you will never be disappointed. As you begin your career or continue with further schooling, know that every area of your life is of interest to Me. You can bring any concern to Me—there is nothing too small or too great. I will be there to help you in your work or to focus your thoughts on that big exam. Don't look to the left or the right. Stay on course. I want only the very best for you. I have a good future for you. Claim it. Walk with Me.

Jesus, keep me on the narrow path
that leads to righteousness. Amen.

WISDOM IN CHRIST

Teach us how short our lives really are so that we may be wise.
PSALM 90:12 NCV

Your life is not short. You have been blessed with eternal life. You will dwell with Me forever in heaven. But you do have a limited number of days on earth. Every day of your life was ordained for you before your birth. Live your life, and use each day to the full. That way you will not have any regrets. Take advantage of every opportunity to serve others and to do good. Examine yourself and find out what spiritual gifts I have put in you. Then go about using them to bless fellow believers. Look outside the walls of the church also. Feed the hungry. Visit the prisoner. You cannot meet every need, but you can meet the ones that are right before you. You can meet the ones that are brought to your attention. Be wise in your decisions about close relationships. Walk with those with whom you are spiritually equally yoked. Be in the world—in the midst of sinners, and shine your light. Yet be not of the world. Resist its temptations through the strength you find in My name. Walk in the wisdom I will pour out upon you, if only you will ask.

Lord, help me to live this day
and every day for You. Amen.

JESUS LIVES WITHIN YOU

Here I am! I stand at the door and knock. If you
hear my voice and open the door, I will come in
and eat with you, and you will eat with me.
REVELATION 3:20 NCV

I waited for you. I did not push My way into your heart. I drew you through My Holy Spirit. I wooed you. Then, when the time was right, you invited Me into your heart. It was a sweet invitation that I so gladly accepted. So what does this mean for you? It means that the Living Lord, the Savior of the world, indwells you. Your body is the temple of the Holy Spirit. I make My home in your heart. When you invite a friend into your home, the two of you fellowship together. You share a meal. You talk to each other. You confide in your friend. Behind the closed doors of your home, you may share things with your friend that you don't share with the entire world. The same is true of your relationship with Me. You have asked Me to be Lord of your life, and I am here for you. I want to hear about your day. I want to rest with you. I want to help bear your burdens. I have come into your heart, and I will never leave you or forsake you.

Jesus, thank You for saving me and for living in my heart. Amen.

LOVE

Above all, love each other deeply,
because love covers over a multitude of sins.
1 PETER 4:8 NIV

N o one is perfect. Those that are closest in your life may hurt you the most. They may not even mean to do so. However, love covers a multitude of sins. Consider the love I poured out for you on the cross. I asked if the cup could be taken from Me, if there was another way. When God declared that I must go to the cross, I gladly bore your sin there. My love covered your sin. Because I have first loved you, love others.

Love them in ways they cannot understand. Show grace. When someone does something that stings a bit, remember the sting of death that I felt to My core for you. Show grace. Forgive. It will change you. Bitterness is a virus. It festers. It takes root in your heart and grows deeper and deeper. Like wild ivy, unforgiveness takes over. Dig it up. Root it out with the release that comes through forgiving others. When you don't feel like loving them, love them anyway. Love is not an emotion; it is an action. It has arms and legs. It takes steps. It hugs. It moves forward and releases the past. It is active and alive, not brooding, not dead. Love covers a multitude of sins.

Jesus, help me to forgive others. You have forgiven me and
shown amazing grace in spite of my sinfulness. Amen.

A TIME FOR EVERYTHING

There is an appointed time for everything.
And there is a time for every event under heaven.
ECCLESIASTES 3:1 NASB

There is a time for everything. Everything has its season. If you are in a season of sadness, know that it will not last forever. God's mercies are new every morning. Joy comes in the morning. After you have been sad or grieved for a while, joy will return. There is a time for every human to be born, and also there is appointed a time for each to die. In between, there is life—some good, some bad. I am with you always, though. I am right here through every season. Even when you walk through the valley of the shadow of death, I am with you. There is a time for everything. Take comfort in the fact that you know the One who holds it all in His hands. Remember that old song you sang as a child—"He's got the whole world in His hands. . . ." It is true. I do. I will not look away—not for a minute. Through every season, I will hold you up and go with you.

Thank You, Jesus, that I can count on You in joy
and in sorrow. There is a time for everything, and You,
my Savior, go with me through it all. Amen.

A FRIEND LOVES AT ALL TIMES

A friend loves you all the time, and a
brother helps in time of trouble.
PROVERBS 17:17 NCV

In life, you need friends. It is good to choose for yourself Christian friends who follow hard after Me. You need to have like-minded friends who will support you and who will speak truth into your life as needed. A friend who has Jesus at the center of his or her life is the only type of friend that you want to have in your inner circle. Certainly there is room for all kinds of friends. You should be a friend to the world. I walked and talked with sinners. I went to the home of Zacchaeus when he called out to Me, "Lord! Lord!" But My dearest friends were My twelve disciples. They were close like brothers.

It is also important to be a friend. Are you a friend on whom others know they can count in times of trouble? You may have heard the saying that it takes being a friend in order to have friends. There is some truth to that. Love others well. You will be loved well in return.

Jesus, guide me as I choose my closest friends.
Put people in my life upon whom I can count. Help me,
in turn, to be a trustworthy friend to others. Amen.

BE LIKE JESUS

Whoever says that he lives in God must live as Jesus lived.
1 JOHN 2:6 NCV

W hen I walked on the earth for thirty-three years, I was not only fully man but also fully God. I lived out My life as an example for My followers. I loved. I laughed. I modeled grace. I distributed it freely. I forgave. I rested. I taught. I guided. I was humble, seeking to serve rather than to be served. I saw to the needs of the poor, the children, the widows, and the disabled. I stood strong in the face of temptation. The devil tempted Me in every way that he tempts you. I resisted. You should follow My lead.

Live as I lived. When you see a bracelet that says "WWJD—What would Jesus do?" take a moment to ponder just that. What would I do? Would I look the other way or give to the needy? Would I ignore the little child or stoop to her level and converse with her? Would I honor My parents or treat them poorly? "What would Jesus do?" It is a question that shouldn't be merely seen in bright colors on fun bracelets and catchy neon T-shirts. It is one you should live your life asking every moment of every day.

Lord, help me to be a little bit more like
You with each passing day. Amen.

WISE AND PLEASANT WORDS

*Wise people's minds tell them what to say, and that
helps them be better teachers. Pleasant words are like
a honeycomb, making people happy and healthy.*
PROVERBS 16:23–24 NCV

You may not feel like a teacher, but you are. There are others watching you. As you begin this new phase of your life after graduation, you have younger people in your life who want to follow in your footsteps. They are watching how you make your decisions and how you act. They are listening to how you converse. You are also an example to those who are not as spiritually mature as you are. These people may be family members, friends, or coworkers who are older than you but who are not as far along in their journey with Me. Seek the wisdom that comes from God. Seek it through prayer and through meditation on the Holy Scriptures. I want you to be wise so that you may teach others well through your example and your words.

Speak pleasant words of encouragement. Speak Life over others. When a prayer request is shared with you, stop right then and pray over that person. Let them hear the kindness and compassion with which you pray to the Father for their need. Not only will pleasant words minister to those you speak to, but they will fill you with happiness and health as well.

*Lord, may my words be wise and pleasant so that
I might be an encouragement to others. Amen.*

UNEXPECTED BLESSING

*Then David comforted Bathsheba his wife. He slept with her and
had sexual relations with her. She became pregnant again and had
another son, whom David named Solomon. The Lord loved Solomon.*
2 Samuel 12:24 ncv

When people think of David and Bathsheba, they remember how
David gave in to the temptation to sleep with another man's wife
and then murdered her husband. What a tangled web of deception and sin
it was! Yet when I think of David, I see him differently—he repented.

To repent is to turn from your old ways and ask Me to forgive your sin.
It involves life change. David had to face many consequences for his sin
with Bathsheba, but he also received an unexpected blessing. After losing
their first child, David was granted another child with Bathsheba. This son,
whose name was Solomon, became known as the wisest man who ever
lived.

The lesson here is to turn from sin and repent. The message is one of
hope and second chances. David failed miserably, but God wasn't through
with him. God didn't walk away. There was discipline. There was a time of
mourning. Then David was blessed with an unexpected surprise. Let go of
the past. Walk away from the sin that so entangles your life. Repent. Focus
on the future. I have special blessings for you that you might otherwise
miss.

Thank You, Jesus, for second chances when I repent from sin. Amen.

YOUR LIFE IS AN OFFERING

You are God's children whom he loves, so try to be like him.
Live a life of love just as Christ loved us and gave himself for
us as a sweet-smelling offering and sacrifice to God.
EPHESIANS 5:1–2 NCV

Your life is an offering to Me. What kind of offering do you bring to My throne? I laid down My life for you, modeling a life of sacrifice. Do you sacrifice for others, or have you been looking out for your own needs so intently that you neglect the needs of others? I love to see you growing in the Word. I delight in time spent with you as you call out to Me regarding your needs and your hopes and desires for the future. There is nothing more beautiful to Me than when you are on your knees praying for others. I love to walk and talk with you. Living a life of love is not natural to the man who does not know God, but it becomes, over time, as involuntary as breathing. Kindness becomes your natural response the more time you spend in My presence and in My Word. My heart is always kind toward you. You are My beloved child. Your life is a sweet-smelling offering poured out before Me. I take great delight in you.

Jesus, may my life be an offering worthy of my King. Amen.

USING YOUR SPIRITUAL GIFTS

Each one of us has a body with many parts, and these parts all have different uses. In the same way, we are many, but in Christ we are all one body. Each one is a part of that body, and each part belongs to all the other parts. We all have different gifts, each of which came because of the grace God gave us.
ROMANS 12:4–6 NCV

Not all believers have been given the same gifts. You are uniquely created, and I have gifted you in special ways. Some are gifted in prophecy, while others are teachers or helpers. Some are gifted in serving. Encouragement, leadership, and giving are other gifts that believers may possess. Finally, some Christians have been given a merciful heart.

Whatever your spiritual gifts may be, they are to be used rather than put on a shelf. They are no good to Me if you are not using them for My glory. Use your gifts to build up the Body of Christ, My Church. The Body is one, but it is made up of many. It is just like your body, which has arms and legs, a mouth and fingers—each a part of the whole, but each with a specific purpose. The parts of the body belong to the whole. Use your gifts, which I bestowed upon you out of grace. Serve the Body.

Lord, help me to determine what my spiritual giftings are, and guide me as I seek to use them for You. Amen.

DO NOT LET EVIL DEFEAT YOU

Do not let evil defeat you,
but defeat evil by doing good.
ROMANS 12:21 NCV

It is easy to love when others show you love. It gets harder when you are mistreated. As you move into adulthood, you will encounter different types of people. The safety net of school and family may not be there for you anymore, but I am here. Nothing touches your life that does not first pass through the filter of My fingers. There are hurts you may not understand from your past, and, child, you have not finished suffering. The world is full of letdowns and evil. The prince of darkness still has some power on earth. One day he will be defeated for good. For now, he prowls about like a lion looking for prey. Do not let evil that is done to you cause you to act in evil. I tell you that it is best to turn the other cheek. Let Me handle the punishment for wrongdoing. There will be judgment for evil in the end.

Defeat evil by doing good. Kill them with kindness. Love when others would hate. This kind of love comes only through the power of your Savior within you. I stand ready to help you.

Lord, help me to love those who do evil to me.
Just as You prayed for those who hung You on the cross,
I will choose to pray for my enemies. Amen.

FRIEND OF GOD

While we were God's enemies, he made friends with us through the death of his Son. Surely, now that we are his friends, he will save us through his Son's life. And not only that, but now we are also very happy in God through our Lord Jesus Christ. Through him we are now God's friends again.
ROMANS 5:10–11 NCV

T he Bible declares that through My death upon the cross, you were made a friend of God. Yes, you are a friend of the God who created the universe. He had a plan all along for the sin that He knew man would commit. He knew from the beginning of the world that My death would provide the necessary sacrifice, the shedding of innocent blood that was needed to unite you with Him again.

Some friendships are up and down. You never know if you can count on certain friends. You can always count on God. He is not like shifting shadows. He is steady and consistent. He is faithful by His very nature. He cannot be anything less. Find your joy in life as you walk with God. The Father is in Me, and I am in Him. We are One, the same and yet unique. You are reconciled to a holy God through your faith in Me as Savior. Always remember that He is your best friend.

Jesus, thank You for making a way for me to come before a holy God and be saved. Amen.

SUCCESS

*Commit your actions to the LORD,
and your plans will succeed.*
PROVERBS 16:3 NLT

S eek Me in the morning, and I will be found. Ask Me for wisdom, and I will give it to you. Whatever you do, commit your plans to Me instead of striking out on your own. There are ways that may seem right to you, but if you pray about it and find that there is a roadblock, trust Me.

Trust that I see the big picture. I see your past, present, and future. I will not let you go too far down a path that will lead you astray before I correct you. Sometimes you may find My discipline in your life distasteful. Children do not always like the boundaries established by their parents either, but the limits are for their own good.

Don't wander off on your own in the jungle of life. Stay close to Me. Talk with Me every day. Lay out your plans. Goals are wonderful. But know that if the job is not offered to you or the relationship ends, this does not mean I have left you. My answer may be yes or no. Sometimes My answer is to wait. I will always give you what is best for you.

*Lord, I commit my plans and desires to You.
I trust that what You have for me is always better
than what I could come up with on my own. Amen.*

PRESS ON

*No, dear brothers and sisters, I have not achieved it, but I focus
on this one thing: Forgetting the past and looking forward to what
lies ahead, I press on to reach the end of the race and receive the
heavenly prize for which God, through Christ Jesus, is calling us.*
PHILIPPIANS 3:13 –14 NLT

Forget the past. Don't dwell on the successes or failures of yesterday.
There is no time for that. Instead, press on toward the future. Keep
your eyes on Me. You are running a race. There are obstacles in the way.
There are other runners. There are time constraints. I have great faith in
you. I have begun a good work in you, and I see you growing and learning.
I see you becoming more and more like Me with each passing day. The race
will be smooth at times. You will feel that you are flying! You will see the
heavenly prize so clearly that you can almost reach out and touch it. Other
times you may have to run in darkness. Your feet may be so heavy and your
spirit so burdened that you can hardly put one foot in front of the other.
In those times, you will need to lean a little harder into Me. Call out to Me.
I am running right alongside you. Press on toward the prize to which you
have been called through your Savior. I am calling you onward. You can
do this!

*Jesus, I will keep running the race. Thank You for being my
constant encouragement. I know that my reward will be great. Amen.*